Truth Barriers

Truth Barriers

Poems by
Tomas Tranströmer
Translated and Introduced by
Robert Bly

Sierra Club Books   San Francisco

Copyright © 1980 by Robert Bly
All rights reserved. No part of this book may be reproduced in any form or by any electronic or mechanical means, including information storage and retrieval systems, without permission in writing from the publisher.

This book was originally published in Sweden under the title *Sanningsbarriären* by Bonniers Forlag, Stockholm, in 1978.

Library of Congress Cataloging in Publication Data

Tranströmer, Tomas, 1931-
    Truth barriers.

    English and Swedish.
    Translation of Sanningsbarriären.
    I. Title.
PT9876.3.R3S2513   839.7'174   80-13310
ISBN 0-87156-235-9
ISBN 0-87156-239-1 (pbk.)

Illustrations by Joseph Stubblefield

Printed in the United States of America
10 9 8 7 6 5 4 3 2 1

Contents

The Boundary Between Worlds

I

Tomas Tranströmer's poems are a luminous example of the ability of poetry that inhabits one culture to travel to another culture and arrive. As Tranströmer said in a letter to the Hungarian poets, published in the magazine *Uj Iras* in 1977, "Poetry has an advantage from the start. . . . Poetry requires no heavy, vulnerable apparatus that has to be lugged around, it isn't dependent on temperamental performers, dictatorial directors, bright producers with irresistible ideas." He also remarked: "Poems are active meditations, they want to wake us up, not put us to sleep." At many places I go in this country, I meet people for whom Tranströmer is an awakener. They receive the fragrance of the depth from him; they see the light suddenly released by one of his brief quatrains. His work has become a strong influence now on many younger American poets, and *Ironwood* recently devoted an entire issue to him; it is the first time the American poets have done a Scandinavian poet this honor.*

We might look at three areas in which his work touches ground in Swedish culture before we speak of his place here. Swedish society is most famously a welfare society, *the* welfare society; it is perhaps the first society in history that has had the means to adopt as an ideal the abolition of poverty. But it is also a technological society like ours, and one given to secular solutions. Tranströmer reports how difficult it is in such a society to keep in touch with inner richness. What happens to the "vertical" longings, the longings for the divine? A new poem, called "Below Freezing," published for the first time in this book, brings up this issue. Tranströmer mentioned while I was translating it that it has references to Swedish society.

> *We are at a party that doesn't love us. Finally the party lets its mask fall and shows what it is: a shunting station for freight cars. In the fog cold giants stand on their tracks. A scribble of chalk on cardoors.*
>
> *One can't say it aloud, but there is a lot of repressed violence here. That is why the furnishings seem so heavy.*

* *Ironwood 13;* the letter to the Hungarian poets (translated by Judith Moffett) and the remarks of John Haines, Keith Harrison, and Göran Printz-Pahlson which follow can be found in this issue, which is available from *Ironwood,* Box 40907, Tucson, Arizona 85717.

I

And why it is so difficult to see the other thing present: a
spot of sun that moves over the house walls and slips over
the unaware forest of flickering faces, a biblical saying
never set down: "Come unto me, for I am as full of
contradictions as you."

I work the next morning somewhere else. I drive there in
a hum through the dawning hour which resembles a dark
blue cylinder. Orion hangs over the frost. Children stand in
a silent clump, waiting for the schoolbus, the children no
one prays for. The light grows as gradually as our hair.

"The children no one prays for" is a painful line. He is not coming
down on the side of orthodox Christianity, and yet a part of him is
aware that children are deprived, even endangered, by not being
prayed for. There is more light now than in primitive times, but it
moves over "an unaware forest of flickering faces."

Tranströmer has said that when he first began to write, in the early
Fifties, it still seemed possible to write a nature poem into which
nothing technological entered. Now, he says, he feels that many objects
created by technology have become almost parts of nature; and the
fact that Sweden has a highly developed technology is always visible
in his recent poems. John Haines wrote in *Ironwood*:

Again and again industrial objects collide with or are combined with,
act against or in concert with, the old shapes of nature. We learn of
cicadas "strong as electric razors," of trees that instead of producing
blossoms, threaten to put forth clusters of iron gloves; pollen is "de-
termined to live in asphalt." A house seen from a distance reminds
him in its redness of a bouillon cube; another house, struck by the
evening light, has shot itself in the forehead. A train comes by and
collects faces and portfolios. The poet's wristwatch gleams "with
Time's imprisoned insect." The historical and political content is sel-
dom absent; swept by more than the wind of April, even the grass
whispers, "Amnesty."

His recent poems do not exile technology, nor does technology
dominate and fragment the poem:

and every year the factory buildings go down another
eighth of an inch—the earth is gulping them slowly.

Paws no one can identify leave a print
on the glossiest artifacts dreamed up here . . .

And no one knows what will happen, we only know
the chain breaks and grows back together all the time.

("*Traffic,*" *from* Friends, You Drank Some Darkness)

Some sights brought about by technology help him to see more vividly
a countryside scene.

All at once I notice the hills on the other side of the lake: their
pine has been clear-cut. They resemble the shaved skull-sections
of a patient about to have a brain operation.

Tranströmer's careful attention to some effects of technology may be
one factor that makes his poems able to cross borders of culture.

A third way in which his poems are native creatures of Sweden is
through his holding to place, his dedication to a specific place. Keith
Harrison mentions that "Tranströmer's 'region' is an island in the
archipelago off the east coast of Sweden and he is as deeply attached
to it as Jean Giono to the Vaucluse, as Meridel le Sueur to Minnesota,
as Hardy to 'Wessex,' as Faulkner to Yoknapatawpha County." Tomas' long poem, "Baltics," which Samuel Charters translated so well,
draws its images from the landscape and history of that island, which
is called Runmarö. Tomas' grandfather on his mother's side worked
out of the island as a ship pilot in the archipelago, and the family has
been there for generations.

2

Tomas Tranströmer was born in Stockholm in 1931, on April 15th.
He is an only child. His father and mother divorced when Tomas was
three; he and his mother lived after that in an apartment in the working
class district of Stockholm. That apartment appears in "Preludes,"
published in *Friends, You Drank Some Darkness*. He studied music
and psychology, and still plays the piano enthusiastically, as his poem
on Schubert makes clear.

The early Fifties were a rather formal time, both here and in Sweden,
and he began by writing highly formal poems, all elements measured.
His first book, *17 Poems*, published in 1954, contains several poems
written in classical meters adapted from the Latin. An example is
"Evening-Morning," published along with the Swedish original, in
Friends, You Drank Some Darkness. The Swedish poet and critic
Göran Printz-Pahlson noticed that the first books of Tomas Tranströmer

3

and Geoffrey Hill, which appeared at about the same time, contained many baroque elements in common. Tranströmer's language has gradually evolved into a more spoken Swedish, and he has written both prose poetry and free verse; but, as he remarked during a recent interview published in *Poetry East:*

Often there is a skeleton somewhere in the poem with a regular number of beats and so on in each line. You don't have to know that, but for me it's important.

Perhaps Tranströmer's early poetry could be described as baroque Romantic, with elements visible from both the eighteenth and nineteenth centuries. Like the Romantics, Tranströmer loves to travel, and a chance encounter may evolve into a poem; but Printz-Pahlson notes a crucial difference between his work and that of the Romantics:

The traveler is brought to a halt, and the experience is imprinted with ferocious energy, but not interpreted.

Tranströmer works slowly and steadily on poems, and often writes only seven or eight poems a year. That may be one reason why his poems have so much weight. His first book included only seventeen poems, but people noticed the power of it immediately. While Tranströmer worked at the Roxtuna Prison for Boys, one of the boys carved a figure of Tomas in wood. It shows a skinny, serious man, arms at his side, who holds in one hand a book. We can see the lettering '17 POEMS' on the spine, which the artist made as wide as though it contained both the New and Old Testaments.

After working several years at Roxtuna, he moved with his family to Vasterås, about forty miles west of Stockholm. There he works as a psychologist for a labor organization funded by the State. His work involves helping juvenile delinquents to reenter society, helping persons with physical disabilities to choose a career, and some work with parole offenders and drug rehabilitation. At a reading in New York, a listener asked him how his work had affected his poetry, and the tone seemed to imply that his poetry was infinitely more important than his work. Tranströmer later mentioned how odd it is that so few ask: "How has your poetry affected your work?" He has commented, in an interview with Rochelle Ratner, that he found out that some juvenile delinquents could not straighten out their lives until they could stop using passive syntax, such as "It happened that . . ." or "What happened to me was . . ." It is important for them to be able to say, "I broke the window and crawled in."

4

He still lives in Vasterås, and has two daughters, Paula and Emma, both now in high school. His wife, Monica, finished her training as a nurse a few years ago, and this year has been in charge of a group of Vietnamese refugees resettling in Sweden. He has published since 1954 seven books of poems, and this one, published in Stockholm in 1978, is the eighth. Up to now, we have had in this country only selections of Tranströmer's past work; now we have a chance to see a book just as he put it together.

3

Tranströmer values his poems not so much as artifacts but as meeting places. Images from widely separated worlds meet in his poems. He said (in the letter to the Hungarian poets), "My poems are meeting places. . . . What looks at first like a confrontation turns out to be connection." The recent poem "Street Crossing," publilshed here, describes an encounter between the ancient Swedish earth and a Stockholm street:

> The street's massive life swirls around me;
> it remembers nothing and desires nothing.
> Far under the traffic, deep in earth,
> the unborn forest waits, still, for a thousand years.

He remains "suspended" so as to hear things:

> one evening in June: the transistor told me the latest
> on the Extra Session: Kosygin, Eban.
> One or two thoughts bored their way in despairingly . . . .
>   I saw heard it from a suspension bridge
> together with a few boys. Their bicycles
> buried in the bushes—only the horns
> stood up.

> ("*Going with the Current*," *from* Friends, You Drank
> Some Darkness)

He likes this "suspension," where objects float in a point of view that can't be identified as "Marxist" or "conservative," right or left. During the Sixties many critics in Sweden demanded that each poet commit himself or herself to a Marxist view, or at least concede that documentaries are the only socially useful form of art. Tranströmer has received several attacks for resisting that doctrine. Art still needs the unconscious, he believes; that has not changed; and he believes a poem needs a place for the private, the quirky, the religious, the unexplainable, the human detail that the collective cannot classify. I think the main reason his poems are hearable in our culture is that he is a poet of awakening.

4

This new book brings forward a fresh emphasis: the poems circle in an intense way around the experience of borders, boundaries of nations, the passage from one world to the next, the weighty instant as we wake up and step from the world of dream to this world, the corridors through which the dead invade our world, the intermediate place between life and art, the contrast between Schubert's genius and Schubert, "a plump young man from Vienna" who sometimes "slept with his glasses on."

The book's title, *Sanningsbarriären*, literally "The Truth Barrier," suggests a customs house, or the customs table at an airport. *Sanningsbarriären* also contains a slight pun on the English phrase: "sound barrier." So breaking the truth barrier is something rarely done—we experience the barriers to truth more than truth itself, or so it seems when we appear at the borders. Tranströmer himself has said that truth appears only at the borders.

I'll quote from a few poems to show how these boundaries appear. In "Start of a Late Autumn Novel," which I've already mentioned, Tranströmer, when once inside the uninhabited island house, finds himself neither asleep nor awake:

> *A few books I've just read sail by like schooners on the way*
> *to the Bermuda Triangle, where they will disappear without*
> *a trace.*

This description is rueful and funny. He's right: sometimes we finish a book and can't remember a word. As the poem continues he lies half asleep, and hears a thumping sound outside. He listens to it—it is something being held down by earth. It beats like a heart under a stethoscope; it seems to vanish and return. Or perhaps there is some being inside the wall who is knocking:

> *someone who belongs to the other world, but got left here anyway,*
> *he thumps, wants to go back. Too late. Wasn't on time down*
> *here, wasn't on time up there, didn't make it on board in time.*

6

So apparently a successful passage to the other world and back has to do with timing; the Celtic fairy tales also emphasize that.

The poem ends with his amazement the next morning when he sees an oak branch, and a torn-up tree root, and a boulder. When, in solitude, we see certain objects, they seem to be "left behind when the ship sailed"; Tranströmer says they are monsters from the other world "whom I love."

In the next poem the boundary between worlds becomes the International Date Line, which lies motionless between Samoa and Tonga. By traveling there, he has crossed the line. "Soon fatigue will flow in through the hole burned by the sun." He mentions that his psychic world has never been permanently scarred by a sudden trauma, but on the other hand some constant slow rubbing has worn away a "mysterious smile" that once showed. More recently the same rubbing that erased the "smile" is now rubbing it back in . . . "no one can tell what it will be worth." He experiences it as "somebody who keeps pulling on my arm each time I try to write." Again we feel ourselves at a boundary, being influenced by something on the other side.

The boundary appears in a different way in "Citoyens." Tomas mentions that "Citoyens" contains a dream he had the night after an automobile accident. He can't see well. During the dream Danton appeared, but Tranströmer could only see half his face, as we only see one side of the moon. So each face has a "dark side," invisible to us. Tranströmer feels a heavy ominous weight in his chest, and the years seem to have lost their usual numbers, as years did after the French Revolution, Year, I, Year II, and so on. The alleys where the dreamer walks curve away toward a "waiting room." Tomas once mentioned to me that the room reminded him of the hospital lobby where he waited so often to see his mother while she was dying of cancer. "The waiting room where we all . . ." Here the border comes very close, and he keeps it close by not finishing the sentence.

The longest poem in the book, "The Gallery," draws its images not from dreams but hallucinations. It records a hallucinatory experience Tranströmer had in a motel, on whose walls the faces of former patients and acquaintances appear. The boundary now becomes the line that separates memory from oblivion.

In "From the Winter of 1947" the dead press through into our world, as the stains in wallpaper. "They want to have their portraits painted." And in "Street Crossing," for one second as he crosses a

7

busy Stockholm street, he has the sensation that the street and the earth below it has eyes, and can see him. On the borders is where one finds truths; at either side of the border, in this world or the next, there may be certainties or doctrines but not truths.

> It is so seldom
> that one of us truly sees the other

The labyrinth is an old image of the border between worlds. In certain ancient myths, whenever a labyrinth appears, the watcher knows the other world is near. Sometimes to avoid being eaten by the other world, he or she has to remember the labyrinth dance and dance it. The labyrinth suddenly turns up at the end of "The Gallery":

> He is standing full length in front of a mountain.
> It is more a snailshell than a mountain.
> It is more a house than a snailshell.
> It is not a house but there are many rooms.
> It is indistinct but overpowering.
> Out of it he grows and it grows out of him.
> It is his life, and it is his labyrinth.

A poem called "December Evening '72," not yet published in English, begins:

> Here I come the invisible man, perhaps in the employ
> of some huge Memory that wants to live at this moment. And
>   I drive by
> the white church that's locked up. A saint made of wood is inside,
> smiling helplessly, as if someone had taken his glasses.

The first two lines suggest that Tranströmer as an artist believes himself to be a servant of the Memory. He writes a poem when some huge Memory wants to cross over into this world; and this view of art seems more European than American. Often in America the artist believes his or her job is to tell the truth about one's own life: confessional poetry certainly implies that. Following that concept of art, many workshop poets comb their personal memory and write poems about their childhood, filling the poems with a clutter of detail. This clutter sometimes insures that the piece will remain "a piece of writing" and will not become "a work of art." I feel that "Schubertiana," one of the greatest poems in Tranströmer's new collection, is a meditation on precisely this issue, namely, What is a work of art?

8

He begins the poem by describing New York from an overlook, "where with one glance you take in the houses where eight million human beings live." He mentions subway cars, coffee cups, desks, elevator doors. And yet

> *I know also—statistics to the side—that at this moment in some*
> *room down there Schubert is being played, and for that*
> *person the notes are more real than all the rest.*

And what are notes? When sounds are absorbed and shaped by and inside, say, a string quartet, they contain almost no life stuff. Notes are pure sound vibrations connected apparently to feelings (but not to experiences) that resonate somewhere inside us. During the "Well-Tempered Clavichord" we feel "feelings" that we seem not to have felt in daily life. There is evidently a layer of consciousness that runs alongside our life, above or below, but is not it. Perhaps it is older. Certain works of art make it their aim to rise up and pierce this layer, or layers. Or they open to allow "memories" from this layer in. Tranströmer has the odd sense that these memories can only come in one by one. While on guard duty in a defense unit a few years ago, he wrote:

> *Task: to be where I am.*
> *Even when I'm in this solemn and absurd*
> *role: I am still the place*
> *where creation does some work on itself.*
>
> *Dawn comes, the sparse tree trunks*
> *take on color now, the frostbitten*
> *forest flowers form a silent search arty*
> *after something that has disappeared in the dark.*
>
> *But to be where I am . . . and to wait:*
> *I am full of anxiety, obstinate, confused.*
> *Things not yet happened are already here!*
> *I feel that. They're just out there:*
> *a murmuring mass outside the barrier.*
> *They can only slip in one by one.*
> *They want to slip in. Why? They do*
> *one by one. I am the turnstile.*

> ("*Sentry Duty*," *from* Friends, You Drank Some
> Darkness)

9

So some European artists—Pasternak and Akhmatova come especially to mind—keep the poem spare and clear so it can pierce the layers.

The art of Schubert puts Tranströmer at a boundary between worlds, and at such a boundary, he sees astonishing truths:

> *The five instruments play. I go home through warm woods*
> *where the earth is springy under my feet*
> *curl up like someone still unborn, sleep, roll on so weightlessly*
> *into the future, suddenly understand that plants are thinking.*

Art helps us, he says, as a banister helps the climber on a dark stairwell. The banister finds its own way in the dark. In certain pieces of music happiness and suffering weigh exactly the same. The depths are above us and below us at the same instant. The melody line is a stubborn

> *humming sound that this instant is with us*
> *upward into*
> *the depths.*

Robert Bly

I

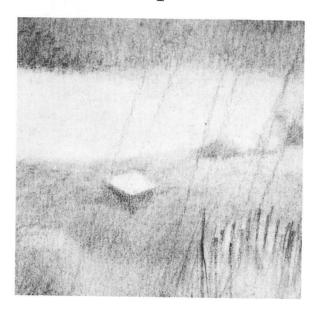

Citoyens

The night after the accident I dreamt of a pockmarked
   man
who walked along alleys singing.
Danton!
Not the other one—Robespierre took no such walks.
He spent one hour each day
on his morning toilette, the rest he gave to the People.
In the heaven of broadsides, among the machines of
   virtue.
Danton
(or the man who wore his mask)
seemed to stand on stilts.
I saw his face from underneath:
like the pitted moon, half lit, half in mourning.
I wanted to say something.
A weight in the chest: the lead weight
that makes the clocks go,
makes the hands go around: Year I, Year II . . .
A pungent odor as from sawdust in tigercages.
And—as always in dreams—no sun.
But the alley walls
shone as they curved away
down toward the waiting-room, the curved space,
the waiting-room where we all . . .

Street Crossing

Cold winds hit my eyes, and two or three suns
dance in the kaleidoscope of tears, as I cross
this street I know so well,
where the Greenland summer shines from snowpools.

The street's massive life swirls around me;
it remembers nothing and desires nothing.
Far under the traffic, deep in earth,
the unborn forest waits, still, for a thousand years.

It seems to me that the street can see me.
Its eyesight is so poor the sun itself
is a gray ball of yarn in black space.
But for a second I am lit. It sees me.

The Clearing

In the middle of the forest there's an unexpected clearing which can only be found by those who have gotten lost.

The clearing is surrounded by a forest that is choking itself. Black trunks with the lichen's bristly beard. The jammed trees are dead all the way to the top, there a few solitary green branches touch the light. Underneath: shadows sitting on shadows, the marsh increasing.

But in the clearing the grass is curiously green and alive. Big stones lie around as if placed that way. They must have been foundation stones for a house, maybe I'm wrong. Who lived there? No one can help with that. The name sleeps somewhere in the archive no one opens (only archives remain young). The oral tradition is dead, and with it the memories. The gypsy tribe remembers, but those who can write forget. Write it down and forget it.

This little house hums with voices. It is the center of the world. But the people in it die or move away. The history ends. The place stands empty year after year. And the crofter's house becomes a sphinx. At the end everything has gone away except the foundation stones.

I've been here before somehow, but it's time to leave. I dive in among the briary underbrush. To get through it you have to take one step forward and two steps to the side, like a chess piece. Slowly it thins out and the light increases. My steps grow longer. A path wiggles its way toward me. I am back in the communications net.

On the humming high voltage pole a beetle sits in the sun. Under his gleaming shoulders his flight wings are lying, folded as ingeniously as a parachute packed by an expert.

Start of a Late Autumn Novel

The boat has the smell of oil, and something whirrs all the time like an obsessive thought. The spotlight is turned on. We are approaching the pier. I'm the only one who is to get off here. "Would you like the gangplank?" No. I take a wobbly step right out into the night, and find myself standing on the pier, on the island. I feel soggy and unwieldy, a butterfly just crept from the cocoon, the plastic clothes-bags in my hands like misshapen wings. I turn and watch the boat go away with its lit windows, then grope my way up to the house I know so well that has been empty. All the houses at this landing are empty now . . . It is lovely to sleep here. I lie on my back, unsure if I'm asleep or awake. A few books I've just read sail by like schooners on the way to the Bermuda Triangle, where they will disappear without a trace. I hear a sound, reverberating, like a drum with poor memory. A thing that the wind thumps again and again against some other object that the earth is holding tight. If the night is not just the absence of light, if night really *is* something, it has to be this sound. The sound of a slow heart heard through the stethoscope, it beats, falls silent a moment, comes back. As if its being went in a zig-zag over the Border. Possibly someone is there, inside the wall, thumping, someone who belongs to the other world, but got left here anyway, he thumps, wants to go back. Too late. Wasn't on time down here, wasn't on time up there, didn't make it on board in time . . . The other world is also this one. The next morning I see a rustly branch with gold and brown leaves hanging on. A root body thrown upward. Stones with faces. The forest is full of monsters that I love left behind when the ship sailed.

For Mats and Laila

The International Date Line lies motionless between
Samoa and Tonga, but the Midnight Line slips forward
over the ocean, over the islands and the hutroofs. On the
other side they are asleep now. Here in Värmland it is
noon, a hot day in late spring . . . I've thrown away my
luggage. A dip in the sky, how blue it is . . . All at once I
notice the hills on the other side of the lake: their pine has
been clear–cut. They resemble the shaved skull-sections of
a patient about to have a brain operation. The shaved hills
have been there all the time; I never noticed them until
now. Blinders and a stiff neck . . . The travel is still going
on. Now the hillsides are full of lines and dark scratches,
as on those old engravings where human beings move
about tiny among the foothills and mountains that
resemble anthills and the villages that are thousands of
lines also. And each human ant carries his own line to the
big engraving; it has no real center, but is alive every-
where. One other thing: the human shapes are tiny
and yet each has its own face, the engraver has allowed
them that, no, they are not ants at all. Most of them are
simple people but they can write their names. Proteus by
comparison is a contemporary individual and he expresses
himself fluently in all styles, comes with a message
"straight from the shoulder," or one in a flowery style,
depending on which gang he belongs to just now. But he
can't write his own name. He draws back from that
terrified, as the wolf from the silver bullet. They're not too
wild for that, the many-headed corporation doesn't want

16

that either, nor the many-headed State . . . The travel keeps going on. In the house over there a man lived who got desperate one afternoon and shot a hole in the empty hammock that was floating over the lawn. And the Midnight Line is getting close, soon it will have completed half its course. (Now don't come and ask me if I want the clock turned back!) Soon fatigue will flow in through the hole burned by the sun . . . It has never happened to me that the diamond of a certain instant cut a permanent scar on my picture of the world. No, it was the wearing, the incessant wearing away that rubbed out the light and somewhat strange smile. But something is about to become visible again, the rubbing brings it *out* this time, it is starting to resemble a smile, but no one can tell what it will be worth. Not clear yet. It is somebody who keeps pulling on my arm each time I try to write.

From the Winter of 1947

Daytime at school: the somber swarming fortress.
In the dusks I went home under signboards.
Then the whispering without lips: "Wake up,
    sleepwalker!"
And all the things were pointing to the Room.

Fifth floor, facing the back yard.
The lamp burned in a terror circle every night.
I sat without eyelids in my bed, watching
the thoughts of the insane run on video tape.

As if this had to be . . .
As if my last childhood had to be smashed
into pieces so it could pass through the bars . . .
As if this had to be . . .

I read books of glass but see only the Other.
The stains that pushed their way through the wallpaper!
Those stains were the dead still alive
who wanted to have their portraits painted.

Until dawn, when the garbagemen arrived
and started banging cans five floors down.
Those peaceful bells of the alley
sent me each morning off to sleep . . .

II

Schubertiana

I

Outside New York, a high place where with one glance
  you take in the houses where eight million human
  beings live.
The giant city over there is a long flimmery drift,
  a spiral galaxy seen from the side.
Inside the galaxy, coffee cups are being pushed across
  the desk, department store windows beg, a whirl of
  shoes that leave no trace behind.
Fire escapes climbing up, elevator doors that silently
  close, behind triple-locked doors a steady swell
  of voices.
Slumped-over bodies doze in subway cars, catacombs in
  motion.
I know also—statistics to the side—that at this instant
  in some room down there Schubert is being played,
  and for that person the notes are more real than
  all the rest.

II

The immense treeless plains of the human brain have
  gotten folded and refolded 'til they are the size of a fist.
The swallow in April returns to its last year's nest
  under the eaves in precisely the right barn in precisely
  the right township.
She flies from the Transvaal, passes the equator,
  flies for six weeks over two continents, navigates
  toward precisely this one disappearing dot in the
  landmass.

And the man who gathers up the signals from a whole
     lifetime into a few rather ordinary chords for five
     string musicians
the one who got a river to flow through the eye of a needle
is a plump young man from Vienna, his friends called
     him "The Mushroom," who slept with his glasses on
and every morning punctually stood at his high writing
     table.
When he did that the wonderful centipedes started to move
     on the page.

III

The five instruments play. I go home through warm
     woods where the earth is springy under my feet,
curl up like someone still unborn, sleep, roll on so
     weightlessly into the future, suddenly understand
     that plants are thinking.

IV

How much we have to take on trust every minute we
     live in order not to drop through the earth!
Take on trust the snow masses clinging to rocksides
     over the town.
Take on trust the unspoken promises, and the smile
     of agreement, trust that the telegram does not concern us,
     and that the sudden ax blow from inside is not coming.

Trust the axles we ride on down the thruway among the
     swarm of steel bees magnified three hundred times.
But none of that stuff is really worth the trust we have.
The five string instruments say that we can take something
     else on trust, and they walk with us a bit on the road.
As when the light bulb goes out on the stair, and the
     hand follows—trusting it—the blind banister rail that
     finds its way in the dark.

          V
We crowd up onto the piano stool and play four-handed
     in f-minor, two drivers for the same carriage, it looks
     a little ridiculous.
It looks as if the hands are moving weights made of sound
     back and forth, as if we were moving lead weights
in an attempt to alter the big scale's frightening balance:
     happiness and suffering weigh exactly the same.
Annie said, "This music is so heroic," and she is right.
But those who glance enviously at men of action, people
     who despise themselves inside for not being murderers,
do not find themselves in this music.
And the people who buy and sell others, and who believe
     that everyone can be bought, don't find themselves here.

Not their music. The long melody line that remains
    itself among all its variations, sometimes shiny and
    gentle, sometimes rough and powerful, the snail's
    trace and steel wire.
The stubborn humming sound that this instant is with us
upward into
the depths:

III

The Gallery

I spent the night at a motel on the freeway.
My room had a smell I had known before
the part of the museum that had the Asian collection:

Tibetan and Japanese masks on a white wall.

This time it isn't masks but faces

that push their way through the white wall of forgetfulness
in order to breathe, ask me about something.
I lie awake and watch them fight
and vanish and return.

Some borrow features from another, switch faces
deep inside me
where forgetfulness and memory make their deals.

They push their way through the second coat of
        forgetfulness
the white wall
they vanish and return.

Here is a sorrow that won't call itself sorrow.

Welcome to the true galleries!
Welcome to the true galleys!
The true gaol-bars!

The karate boy who paralyzed a man
goes on dreaming of quick profits.

That woman keeps buying more and more things
in order to throw them into the jaw of Nothing
that wiggles around behind her.

Mr. X doesn't dare to leave his room.
A dark stockade of equivocal people
stands between him
and the steadily disappearing horizon.

This one escaped from Karelia
and was able to laugh then . . .
She reappears now
but dumb, petrified, a statue from Sumeria.

As when I was ten years old and came home late.
The lamps were out on the stair
but the elevator where I stood had lights and it rose
like a diver's bell through black depths
floor after floor while imaginary faces
pressed against the bars . . .

But these faces are not imagined, they are real.

I lie stretched out like a cross-street.

Many people climb up from the white mist.
We managed to touch one another, once, we did!

A long lit corridor that reeks of carbolic acid.
A wheelchair. The teen-age girl
learning to talk after the carcrash.

The man who tried to shout under the water
and the world's chill mass forced its way in
through his nose and mouth.

Voices spoke into the microphone: speed is power
speed is power
Start it rolling, the show must go on!

Following our career we walk stiffly step by step
as in a no-play
with masks, a high-pitched singing: here I am, here I am!
The loser
is represented by a rolled-up blanket.

One artist said: when younger I was a planet
with its own dense atmosphere.
The descending rays of light broke into rainbows.
Constant thunderstorms raged inside . . .

Now I am extinct and dry and opened.
I lack a certain childlike energy.
I have a hot side and a cold side.

But no rainbows.

I spent the night in the thin-walled house.
Many others wanted to penetrate the walls
but most of them can't make it.

They are shouted down by the white noise of forgetfulness.

Anonymous songs of the drowned in the walls.
Modest rappers who wish not to be heard
long long sighs
my old replies that creep around homeless.

Hear society's mechanical self-attacks
voices like large fans
the artificial wind in the mine tunnels
1800 feet down.

Under the bandages our eyes remain open.

If at least I could just get them to grasp
that this quivering underneath us
means that we are walking on a bridge . . .

Often I have to stand absolutely still.
I am the knife-thrower's partner!
Questions that in a rage I tossed out
come whizzing back

not piercing me but nailing my outline down firmly
A rough outline
When I have left the spot it stays there.

Often I have to say nothing. Voluntarily!
Because the "last word" can be spoken again and again.
Because hello and goodbye . . .
Because this day that has at last come today . . .

Because the margins eventually will rebel
overflow their banks
and flood the texts.

I stayed over in the sleepwalker's motel.
Many faces here are in despair
others flattened
after their pilgrim's walk through forgetting.

They breathe vanish fight their way back
looking beyond me
they all want to reach the icon of justice.

It is so seldom
that one of us truly *sees* the other:

for a fraction of a second as in a photograph
a man appears but sharper
and behind him
something that is bigger than his shadow.

He is standing full length in front of a mountain.
It is more a snailshell than a mountain.
It is more a house than a snailshell.
It is not a house but there are many rooms.
It is indistinct but overpowering.
Out of it he grows and it grows out of him.
It is his life, and it is his labyrinth.

IV

Below Freezing

We are at a party that doesn't love us. Finally the party lets the mask fall and shows what it is: a shunting station for freight cars. In the fog cold giants stand on their tracks. A scribble of chalk on cardoors.

One can't say it aloud, but there is a lot of repressed violence here. That is why the furnishings seem so heavy. And why it is so difficult to see the other thing present: a spot of sun that moves over the house walls and slips over the unaware forest of flickering faces, a biblical saying never set down: "Come unto me, for I am as full of contradictions as you."

I work the next morning somewhere else. I drive there in a hum through the dawning hour which resembles a dark blue cylinder. Orion hangs over the frost. Children stand in a silent clump, waiting for the schoolbus, the children no one prays for. The light grows as gradually as our hair.

Boat, Town

A Portuguese fishing boat, blue, the wake rolls back the
    Atlantic always.
A blue dot far out, but still I am there—the six on board
    do not notice that we are seven.

I saw a boat like that being built, it lay like a huge lute
    without strings
in the Gap of the Poor, the town where women keep
    washing and washing in rage, in patience, in sadness.

People blackened the beach. It was a rally just breaking up,
    loudspeakers being carried away.
Military police escorted the speaker's Mercedes through
    the crowd, words hit the steel carsides.

Montenegro

At the next bend the bus broke free from the cold
   mountain shadow,
turned its nose toward the sun, and crept in a roar upward.
We were all cramped. The dictator's bust was present too,
wrapped in newspaper. A bottle went from mouth to
   mouth.
The birthmark of death grows at a different pace with each
   of us.
Up on top the blue sea caught up with the sky.

Calling Home

A telephone call flowed out into the night, and it gleamed
   here and there in fields, and at the outskirts of cities.

Afterward I slept restlessly in the hotel bed.

I resembled the compass needle the orienteer runner
   carries as he runs with heart pounding.

After a Long Dry Spell

The summer is gray now strange evening.
Rain creeps down from the sky
and lands on the field silently
as if it intended to overpower a sleeper.

Circles swarm on the fjord's surface
and that is the only surface there is right now—
the rest is highth and depth
to rise and to sink.

Two pine trunks
shoot up and continue in long hollow signal-drums.
Cities and the sun gone off.
In the high grass there is thunder.

It's OK to telephone the island that is a mirage.
It's OK to listen to the gray voice.
To thunder iron ore is honey.
It's OK to live by your own code.

A Place in the Woods

On the way there a couple of startled wings fluttered, and
that was all. One goes there alone. It is a lofty building
made entirely of open spaces, a building which sways all
the time, but is never able to fall. The sun, changed into
a thousand suns, drifts in through the open slivers. And
an inverse law of gravity takes hold in the play of light:
this house floats anchored in the sky, and what falls falls
upward. It makes you turn around. In the woods it is all
right to grieve. It's all right to see the old truths, which
we usually keep packed away in the luggage. My roles
down there in the deep places fly up, hang like dried
skulls in an ancestor hut on a remote Melanesian island.
A childlike light around the terrifying trophies. Woods
are mild that way.

At Funchal

(Island of Madeira)

On the beach there's a seafood place, simple, just a shack thrown up by survivors of the shipwreck. Many turn back at the door, but not the sea winds. A shadow stands deep inside his smoky hut frying two fish according to an old recipe from Atlantis, tiny garlic explosions, oil running over sliced tomatoes, every morsel says that the ocean wishes us well, a humming from the deep places.

She and I look into each other. It's like climbing the wild-flowered mountain slopes without feeling the least bit tired. We've sided with the animals, they welcome us, we don't age. But we have experienced so much together over the years, including those times when we weren't so good (as when we stood in line to give blood to the healthy giant—he said he wanted a transfusion), incidents which should have separated us if they hadn't united us, and incidents which we've totally forgotten—though they haven't forgotten us! They've turned to stones, dark and light, stones in a scattered mosaic. And now it happens: the pieces move toward each other, the mosaic reappears, whole. It waits for us. It glows down from the hotel room wall, some figure violent and tender, perhaps a face, we can't take it all in as we pull off our clothes.

After dusk we go out. The dark powerful paw of the cape lies thrown out into the sea. We walk in swirls of human beings, we are cuffed around kindly, among soft tyrannies . . . everyone chatters excitedly in the foreign tongue. "No man is an island." We gain strength from *them,* but also from ourselves. From what is inside that the other person can't see. That which can only meet itself. The innermost paradox, the underground garage flowers, the vent toward the good dark. A drink that bubbles in empty glasses. An amplifier that magnifies silence. A path that grows over after every step. A book that can only be read in the dark.

Sanningsbarriären: Original Swedish Texts

Citoyens

Natten efter olyckan drömde jag om en koppärrig man
som gick och sjöng i gränderna.
Danton!
Inte den andre—Robespierre tar inte såna promenader.
Robespierre gör omsorgsfull toalett en timme på morgonen,
resten av dygnet ägnar han åt Folket.
I pamfletternas paradis, bland dygdens maskiner.
Danton—
eller den som bar hans mask—
stod som på styltor.
Jag såg hans ansikte underifrån:
som den ärriga månen,
till hälften i ljus, till hälften i sorg.
Jag ville säga något.
En tyngd i bröstet, lodet
som får klockorna att gå,
visarna att vrida sig: år 1, år 2 . . .
En frän doft som från sågspånen i tigerstallarna.
Och—som alltid i drömmen—ingen sol.
Men murarna lyste
i gränderna som krökte sig
ner mot väntrummet, det krökta rummet,
väntrummet där vi alla . . .

Övergångsstället

Isblåst mot ögonen och solarna dansar
i tårarnas kaleidoskop när jag korsar
gatan som följt mig så länge, gatan
där grönlandssommaren lyser ur pölarna.

Omkring mig svärmar gatans hela kraft
som ingenting minns och ingenting vill.
I marken djupt under trafiken väntar
den ofödda skogen stilla i tusen år.

42

Jag får den idén att gatan ser mig.
Dess blick är så skum att solen själv
blir ett grått nystan i en svart rymd.
Men just nu lyser jag! Gatan ser mig.

Gläntan

Det finns mitt i skogen en oväntad glänta som bara kan hittas av den
som gått vilse.

Gläntan är omsluten av en skog som kväver sig själv. Svarta
stammar med lavarnas askgrå skäggstubb. De tätt sammanskruvade
träden är döda ända upp i topparna där några enstaka gröna kvistar
vidrör ljuset. Därunder: skugga som ruvar på skugga, kärret som
växer.

Men på den öppna platsen är gräset underligt grönt och levande.
Här ligger stora stenar, liksom ordnade. De måste vara grundstenarna
i ett hus, jag kanske tar fel. Vilka levde här? Ingen kan ge upplysning
om det. Namnen finns någonstans i ett arkiv som ingen öppnar (det är
bara arkiven som håller sig unga). Den muntliga traditionen är död
och därmed minnena. Zigenarstammen minns men de skrivkunniga
glömmer. Anteckna och glöm.

Torpet sorlar av röster, det är världens centrum. Men invånarna
dör eller flyttar ut, krönikan upphör. Det står öde i många år. Och
torpet blir en sfinx. Till slut är allt borta utom grundstenarna.

På något sätt har jag varit här förut, men måste gå nu. Jag dyker in
bland snåren. Det går bara att tränga sig igenom med ett steg framåt
och två åt sidan, som en schackspringare. Så småningom glesnar det
och ljusnar. Stegen blir längre. En gångstig smyger sig fram till mig.
Jag är tillbaka i kommunikationsnätet.

På den nynnande kraftledningsstolpen sitter en skalbagge i solen.
Under de glänsande sköldarna ligger flygvingarna hopvecklade lika
sinnrikt som en fallskärm packad av en expert.

Början på Senhöstnattens Roman

Passagerarbåten luktar olja och nånting skallrar hela tiden som en tvångstanke. Strålkastaren tänds. Vi närmar oss bryggan. Det är bara jag som ska av här. "Behöveru landgången?" Nej. Jag tar ett långt vacklande kliv rätt in i natten och står på bryggan, på ön. Jag känner mig blöt och ovig, en fjäril som just krupit ur puppskalet, plastpåsarna i vardera handen hänger som missbildade vingar. Jag vänder mig om och ser båten blida bort med sina lysande fönster, trevar mig sen fram till huset som stått tomt så länge. Alla hus i grannskapet står obebodda . . . Det är skönt att somna in här. Jag ligger på rygg och vet inte om jag sover eller är vaken. Några böcker jag läst passerar förbi som gamla seglare på väg till Bermuda-triangeln för att försvinna utan spår . . . Det hörs ett ihåligt ljud, en tankspridd trumma. Ett föremål som blåsten åter och åter dunkar mot något som jorden håller stilla. Om natten inte bara är frånvaron av ljus, om natten verkligen *är* något, så är den detta ljud. Stetoskopljuden från ett långsamt hjärta, det bultar, tystnar ett tag, kommer tillbaka. Som om varelsen rörde sig i sick-sack över Gränsen. Eller någon som bultar i en vägg, någon som hör till den andra världen men blev kvar här, bultar, vill tillbaka. Försent! Hann inte dit ner, hann inte dit upp, hann inte ombord . . . Den andra världen är också den här världen. Nästa morgon ser jag en fräsande gyllenbrun lövruska. En krypande rotvälta. Stenar med ansikten. Skogen är full av akterseglade vidunder som jag älskar.

Till Mats och Laila

Datumlinjen ligger stilla mellan Samoa och Tonga men Midnattslinjen glider fram över oceanen och öarna och hyddornas tak. De sover där, på andra sidan. Här i Värmland är det mitt på dagen, en solbrinnande försommardag—jag har slängt ifrån mig bagaget. En simtur i himlen, vad luften är blå . . . Då ser jag plötsligt åsarna på andra sidan sjön: de är kalhuggna. Liknar de rakade partierna av hjässan på en patient som ska hjärnopereras. Det har funnits där hela tiden, jag såg det inte förrän nu. Skygglappar och nackspärr . . . Resan fortsätter. Nu är landskapet fullt av streck och linjer, som på de gamla gravyrerna där människor rörde sig små

44

mellan kullar och berg som liknade myrstackar och byar som också
var tusentals streck. Och varje människomyra drog sitt streck till den
stora gravyren, det fanns inget riktigt centrum men allt levde. En
annan sak: figurerna är små men de har alla ett eget ansikte, gravören
har unnat dem det, nej de är inga myror. De flesta är enkla människor
men de kan skriva sitt namn. Proteus däremot är en modern människa
och uttrycker sig flytande i alla stilar, kommer med "raka budskap"
eller krusiduller, beroende på vilket gäng han tillhör just nu. Men han
kan inte skriva sitt namn. Han ryggar tillbaka för det som varulven
för silverkulan. Det kräver de inte heller, inte bolagshydran, inte
Staten . . . Resan fortsätter. I det här huset bor en man som blev
desperat en kväll och sköt skarpt mot den tomma hängmattan som
svävade över gräset. Och midnattslinjen närmar sig, den har snart gått
halva varvet runt. (Kom inte och påstå att jag vill vrida klockan
tillbaka!) Tröttheten ska strömma in genom hålet som blev efter solen
. . . Aldrig var jag med om att ett visst ögonblicks diamant drog en
outplånlig repa tvärs över världsbilden. Nej det var nötningen, den
ständiga nötningen som suddade ut det ljusa främmande leendet. Men
något håller på att bli synligt igen, det håller på att *nötas* fram, börjar
likna ett leende, man vet inte vad det kan vara värt. Ouppklarat. Det
är någon som hugger tag i min arm varje gång jag försöker skriva.

Från Vintern 1947

Om dagarna i skolan den dova myllrande fästningen.
I skymningen gick jag hem under skyltarna.
Då kom viskningen utan läppar: "Vakna sömngångare!"
och alla föremål pekade mot Rummet.

Femte våningen, rummet mot gården. Lampan brann
i en cirkel av skräck alla nätter.
Jag satt utan ögonlock i sängen och såg
bildband bildband med de sinnessjukas tankar.

Som om det var nödvändigt . . .
Som om den sista barndomen slogs sönder
för att kunna passera genom gallret.
Som om det var nödvändigt . . .

Jag läste i böcker av glas men såg bara det andra:
fläckarna som trängde fram genom tapeterna.
Det var de levande döda
som ville ha sina porträtt målade!

Tills gryningen då sophämtarna kom
och slamrade med plåtkärlen där nere
bakgårdens fridfulla grå klockor
som ringde mig till sömns.

Schubertiana

I

I kvällsmörkret på en plats utanför New York, en utsiktspunkt där
man med en enda blick kan omfatta åtta miljoner människors hem.
Jättestaden där borta är en lång flimrande driva, en spiralgalax från
sidan.
Inne i galaxen skjuts kaffekoppar över disken, skyltfönstren tigger av
förbipasserande, ett vimmel av skor som inte sätter några spår.
De klättrande brandstegarna, hissdörrarna som glider ihop, bakom
dörrar med polislås ett ständigt svall av röster.
Hopsjunkna kroppar halvsover i tunnelbanevagnarna, de
framrusande katakomberna.
Jag vet också—utan all statistik—att just nu spelas Schubert i något
rum därborta och att för någon är de tonerna verkligare än allt det
andra.

II

Människohjärnans ändlösa vidder är hopskrynklade till en knytnäves
storlek.
I april återvänder svalan till sitt fjolårsbo under takrännan på just den
ladan i just den socknen.
Hon flyger från Transvaal, passerar ekvatorn, flyger under sex veckor
över två kontinenter, styr mot just denna försvinnande prick i
landmassan.
Och han som fångar upp signalerna från ett helt liv i några ganska
vanliga ackord av fem stråkar

46

han som får en flod att strömma genom ett nålsöga
är en tjock yngre herre från Wien, av vännerna kallad
    "Svampen", som sov med glasögonen på
och ställde sig punktligt vid skrivpulpeten om morgonen.
Varvid notskriftens underbara tusenfotingar satte sig i rörelse.

III
De fem stråkarna spelar. Jag går hem genom ljumma skogar med
    marken fjädrande under mig
kryper ihop som en ofödd, somnar, rullar viktlös in i framtiden,
    känner plötsligt att växterna har tankar.

IV
Så mycket vi måste lita på för att kunna leva vår dagliga dag utan att
    sjunka genom jorden!
Lita på snömassorna som klamrar sig fast vid bergssluttningen
    ovanför byn.
Lita på tysthetslöftena och samförståndsleendet, lita på att
    olyckstelegrammen inte gäller oss och att det plötsliga yxhugget
    inifrån inte kommer.
Lita på hjulaxlarna som bär oss på motorleden mitt i den trehundra
    gånger förstorade bisvärmen av stål.
Men ingenting av det där är egentligen värt vårt förtroende.
De fem stråkarna säger att vi kan lita på någonting annat och de följer
    oss en bit på väg dit.
Som när ljuset slocknar i trappan och handen följer—med
    förtroende—den blinda ledstången som hittar i mörkret.

V
Vi tränger ihop oss framför pianot och spelar med fyra händer i
    fmoll, två kuskar på samma ekipage, det ser en aning löjligt ut.
Händerna tycks flytta klingande vikter fram och tillbaka, som om vi
    rörde motvikterna
i ett försök att rubba den stora vågarmens ohyggliga balans: glädje
    och lidande väger precis lika.
Annie sa "den här musiken är så heroisk", och det är sant.

Men de som sneglar avundsjukt på handlingens män, de som innerst
   inne föraktar sig själva för att de inte är mördare
de känner inte igen sig här.
Och de många som köper och säljer människor och tror att alla kan
   köpas, de känner inte igen sig här.
Inte deras musik. Den långa melodin som är sig själv i alla
   förvandlingar, ibland glittrande och vek, ibland skrovlig och stark,
   snigelspår och stålwire.
Det envisa gnolandet som följer oss just nu
uppför
djupen.

Galleriet

Jag låg över på ett motell vid E 3.
I mitt rum där fanns en lukt som jag känt förut
bland de asiatiska samlingarna på ett museum:

masker tibetanska japanska mot en ljus vägg.

Men det är inte masker nu utan ansikten

som tränger fram genom glömskans vita vägg
för att andas, för att fråga om något.
Jag ligger vaken och ser dem kämpa
och försvinna och återkomma.

Några lånar drag av varann, byter ansikten
långt inne i mig
där glömska och minne bedriver sin kohandel.

De tränger fram genom glömskans övermålning
den vita väggen
de försvinner och återkommer.

Här finns en sorg som inte kallar sig så.

Välkommen till de autentiska gallerierna!
Välkommen till de autentiska galärerna!
De autentiska gallren!

Karatepojken som slog en människa lam
drömmer fortfarande om snabba vinster.

Den här kvinnan köper och köper saker
för att kasta i gapet på tomrummen
som smyger bakom henne.

Herr X vågar inte lämna sin våning.
Ett mörkt staket av mångtydiga människor
står mellan honom
och den ständigt bortrullande horisonten.

Hon som en gång flydde från Karelen
hon som kunde skratta . . .
nu visar hon sig
men stum, förstenad, en staty från Sumer.

Som när jag var tio år och kom sent hem.
I trappuppgången slocknade lamporna
men hissen där jag stod lyste, och hissen steg
som en dykarklocka genom svarta djup
våning för våning medan inbillade ansikten
tryckte sig mot gallret . . .

Men det är inte inbillade ansikten nu utan verkliga.

Jag ligger utsträckt som en tvärgata.

Många stiger fram ur den vita dimman.
Vi rörde vid varann en gång, verkligen!

En lång ljus korridor som luktar karbol.
Rullstolen. Tonårsflickan
som lär sig tala efter bilkraschen.

49

Han som försökte ropa under vattnet
och världens kalla massa trängde in
genom näsa och mun.

Röster i mikrofonen sa: Fart är makt
fart är makt!
Spela spelet, the show must go on!

I karriären rör vi oss stelt steg för steg
som i ett no-spel
med masker, skrikande sång: Jag, det är Jag!
Den som slogs ut
representerades av en hoprullad filt.

En konstnär sa: Förr var jag en planet
med en egen tät atmosfär.
Strålarna utifrån bröts där till regnbågar.
Ständiga åskvädar rasade inom, inom.

Nu är jag slocknad och torr och öppen.
Jag saknar numera barnslig energi.
Jag har en het sida och en kall sida.

Inga regnbågar.

Jag låg över i det lyhörda huset.
Många vill komma in där genom väggarna
men de flesta tar sig inte ända fram:

de överröstas av glömskans vita brus.

Anonym sång drunknar i väggarna.
Försynta knackningar som inte vill höras
utdragna suckar
mina gamla repliker som kryper hemlösa.

Hör samhällets mekaniska självförebråelser
stora fläktens röst

som den konstgjorda blåsten i gruvgångarna
sexhundra meter nere.

Våra ögon står vidöppna under bandagen.

Om jag åtminstone kunde få dem att känna
att den här skälvningen under oss
betyder att vi är på en bro . . .

Ofta måste jag stå alldeles orörlig.
Jag är knivkastarens partner på cirkus!
Frågor jag slängt ifrån mig i raseri
kommer vinande tillbaka

träffar inte men naglar fast min kontur
i grova drag
sitter kvar när jag har gått från platsen.

Ofta måste jag tiga. Frivilligt!
Därför att "sista ordet" sägs gång på gång.
Därför att goddag och adjö . . .
Därför att den dag som idag är . . .

Därför att marginalerna stiger till sist
över sina bräddar
och översvämmar texten.

Jag låg över på sömngångarnas motell.
Många ansikten härinne är förtvivlade
andra utslätade
efter pilgrimsvandringarna genom glömskan.

De andas försvinner kämpar sig tillbaka
de ser förbi mig
de vill alla fram till rättvisans ikon.

Det händer men sällan
att en av oss verkligen *ser* den andre:

ett ögonblick visar sig en människa
som på ett fotografi men klarare
och i bakgrunden
någonting som är större än hans skugga.

Han står i helfigur framför ett berg.
Det är mera ett snigelskal än ett berg.
Det är mera ett hus än ett snigelskal.
Det är inte ett hus men har många rum.
Det är otydligt men överväldigande.
Han växer fram ur det, och det ur honom.
Det är hans liv, det är hans labyrint.

Minusgrader

Vi är på en fest som inte älskar oss. Till sist låter festen sin mask falla
och visar sig som den verkligen är: en växlingsbangård. Kalla kolosser
står på skenor i dimman. En krita har klottrat på vagnsdörrarna.

Det får inte nämnas, men här finns mycket undertryckt våld. Därför
är detaljerna så tunga. Och så svårt att se det andra som också finns:
en solkatt som flyttar sig på husväggen och glider genom den ovetande
skogen av flimrande ansikten, ett bibelord som aldrig skrevs: "Kom
till mig, ty jag är motsägelsefull som du själv."

I morgon arbetar jag i en annan stad. Jag susar dit genom morgon-
timman som är en stor svartblå cylinder. Orion hänger ovanför
tjälen. Barn står i en tyst klunga och väntar på skolbussen, barn
som ingen ber för. Ljuset växer sakta som vårt hår.

Båten—Byn

En portugisisk fiskebåt, blå, kölvattnet rullar upp Atlanten ett stycke.
En blå punkt långt ute, och ändå ser jag där—de sex ombord märker
   inte att vi är sju.

Jag såg en sån båt byggas, den låg som en stor luta utan strängar
i fattigravinen: byn där man tvättar och tvättar i ursinne, tålamod,
   vemod.

Svart av folk på stranden. Det var ett möte som skingrades,
   högtalarna bars bort.
Soldater ledde talarens mercedes genom trängseln, ord trummade mot
   plåtsidorna.

Svarta Bergen

I nästa kurva kom bussen loss ur bergets kalla skugga
vände nosen mot solen och kröp rytande uppför.
Vi trängdes i bussen. Diktatorns byst var också med
inslagen i tidningspapper. En flaska gick från mun till mun.
Döden födelsemärket växte olika snabbt hos alla.
Uppe i bergen hann det blå havet ikapp himlen.

Hemåt

Ett telefonsamtal rann ut i natten och glittrade på landsbygden och i
   förstäderna.
Efteråt sov jag oroligt i hotellsängen.
Jag liknade nålen i en kompass som orienteringslöparen bär genom
   skogen med bultande hjärta.

53

Efter en Lång Torka

Sommaren är grå just nu underliga kväll.
Regnet smyger ner från himlen
och tar mark stilla
som om det gällde att övermanna en sovande.

Vattenringarna myllrar på fjärdens yta
och det är den enda yta som finns—
det andra är höjd och djup
stiga och sjunka.

Två tallstammar
skjuter upp och fortsätter i långa ihåliga signaltrummor.
Borta är städerna och solen.
Åskan finns i det höga gräset.

Det går att ringa upp hägringens ö.
Det går att höra den gråa rösten.
Järnmalm är honung för åskan.
Det går att leva med sin kod.

Skogsparti

På vägen dit smattrade ett par uppskrämda vingar, det var allt. Dit går
man ensam. Det är en hög byggnad som helt och hållet består av
springor, en byggnad som alltid vacklar men aldrig kan störta. Den
tusenfaldiga solen svävar in genom springorna. I spelet av ljus råder
en omvänd tyngdlag: huset förankras i himlen och det som faller, det
faller uppåt. Där får man vända sig om. Där är det tillåtet att sörja.
Där vågar man se vissa gamla sanningar som annars alltid hålls
nerpackade. Mina roller på djupet, de flyter upp där, hänger som de
torkade skallarna i förfädershyddan på någon melanesisk avkroksö.
En barnslig dager kring de hiskliga troféerna. Så mild är skogen.

54

Funchal

Fiskrestaurangen på stranden, enkel, ett skjul uppfört av skepps-
brutna. Många vänder i dörren men inte vindstötarna från havet.
En skugga står i sin rykande hytt och steker två fiskar enligt ett
gammalt recept från Atlantis, små explosioner av vitlök, olja som
rinner på tomatskivorna. Varje tugga säger att oceanen vill oss väl,
ett nynnande från djupen.

Hon och jag ser in i varann. Som att klättra uppför de vilt
blommande sluttningarna utan att känna den minsta trötthet. Vi är på
djursidan, välkomna, åldras inte. Men vi har upplevt så mycket
tillsammans, det minns vi, också stunder då vi inte var mycket värda
(som när vi köade för att ge den välmående jätten blod—han hade
beordrat transfusion), händelser som skulle ha skilt oss om de inte
hade förenat oss, och händelser som vi glömt tillsammans—men de
har inte glömt oss! De blev stenar, mörka och ljusa. Stenarna i en
förskingrad mosaik. Och nu händer det: skärvorna flyger samman,
mosaiken blir till. Den väntar på oss. Den strålar från väggen i
hotellrummet, en design våldsam och öm, kanske ett ansikte, vi hinner
inte uppfatta allt när vi drar av oss kläderna.

I skymningen går vi ut. Uddens väldiga mörkblå tass ligger slängd i
havet. Vi går in i människovirveln, knuffas omkring vänligt, mjuka
kontroller, alla pratar ivrigt på det främmande språket. "Ingen
människa är en ö." Vi blir starka av *dem*, men också av oss själva. Av
det inom oss som den andre inte kan se. Det som bara kan möta sig
själv. Den innersta paradoxen, garageblomman, ventilen mot det goda
mörkret. En dryck som bubblar i tomma glas. En högtalare som
utsänder tystnad. En gångstig som växer igen bakom varje steg. En
bok som bara kan läsas i mörkret.